secrets of light
latin cooking

by Alexandra Drijanski, Esther Guindi, and Mabel Killer
translated by Mary Humphreys and Susan Lowell

RIO NUEVO PUBLISHERS
P.O. Box 5250
Tucson, AZ 85703-0250
(520) 623-9558
www.rionuevo.com

Originally published in 2002 by Arquitectos Mexicanos Editores
(as **Secretos de la comida sana**), © 2002 Alexandra Drijanski,
Esther Guindi, Mabel Killer.

Translation © 2004 Mary Humphreys and Susan Lowell.

Library of Congress Cataloging-in-Publication Data

Drijanski, Alexandra.
    [Secretos de la comida sana. English]
    Secrets of light Latin cooking / Alexandra Drijanski, Esther Guindi,
Mabel Killer ; translated by Mary Humphreys and Susan Lowell.-- 1st ed.
            p. cm.
Includes index.
    ISBN 1-887896-57-0
 1. Cookery, Latin American. 2. Cookery, Mexican. 3. Low-fat
diet--Recipes. I. Guindi, Esther. II. Killer, Mabel. III. Title.
    TX716.A1D7513 2004
    641.598--dc22
                                                    2003024773
. . . .
Printed in Hong Kong

10 9 8 7 6 5 4 3 2 1

To our husbands and children, for their unconditional support:

Pepe, Regina, and Andrea Mizrahi

Gil, Sonia, and Jack Mussan

Roberto, Julieta, and Laura Vecchiarelli

To Helena Ibarra, a Venezuelan chef with the virtue of true greatness: to share knowledge with complete generosity and selflessness.

good food: the secret is beautiful balance

In our quest for a fuller, happier life, in Latin America as elsewhere, modern society has developed a deeper consciousness of what is natural and healthy. One result is the light, lovely food you will find in this book—along with some of our secrets. Do they include the secret of happiness? Maybe so. Without a doubt, health and happiness are closely related. To feel and look well raises a person's self-esteem, and this leads to better relationships with others.

The challenge today is to find the right nutritional balance, always remembering that "healthy eating" should also mean "delicious food." As you will see, low-fat, lightly sweetened, nutritious dishes can be beautiful to behold and wonderful to eat.

Luckily our world offers us a great variety of foods, and each of these is endowed with a flavor, an aroma, a consistency, and a texture that, along with its nutritional content, make it absolutely unique. Yet in spite of their differences, some foods do share similar characteristics, so we can classify them in three general nutritional categories: **carbohydrates, proteins, and vitamins and minerals.** For our bodies to function well, all three groups are indispensable, and a balanced meal includes at least one food from each classification. For cooks, these groups are the building blocks of savory menus. If you choose one recipe from each section of this book, you will produce a beautifully balanced meal, rich with the bright flavors of modern Latin America. (In the very few recipes with ingredients that are rare in the United States, we have suggested easy substitutions.)

grains and starches (see "Pastas, Potatoes, and Rice")

This group provides carbohydrates and fiber. Carbohydrates mainly supply the energy that fuels the body, providing the power that allows all the organs to work, while fiber helps with digestion.

Foods derived from grains or cereals are: tortillas, corn, bread, crackers, pasta, rice, oats, barley, and even amaranth. Starchy tubers include potatoes, sweet potatoes, yams, and cassava.

foods of animal origin and legumes (see "Fish, Chicken, and Meat")

This group provides protein. Protein is the construction material that helps to repair all the tissues of the body, facilitating cellular regeneration, the growth of hair and nails, and the healing of wounds, among other benefits.

Foods of animal origin are: beef, pork, chicken, turkey, fish, shellfish, eggs, milk, cheese, yogurt, etc. Legumes include: pinto beans, fava beans, lentils, and chickpeas.

fruits and vegetables (see "Fruit Desserts and More" and "Vegetables and More")

This group supplies vitamins and minerals that help to metabolize foods, build immunities, strengthen vision, speed the healing of wounds, and promote the formation of new cells.

Among fruits are found: apples, pears, melons, papayas, mangos, grapes, strawberries, sapodillas, pineapples, oranges, grapefruit, cherries, peaches, bananas, etc. Among vegetables: cucumbers, tomatoes, lettuce, prickly pear pads, asparagus, broccoli, spinach, mushrooms, chayotes. green chiles, tomatillos, squash, cauliflower, and Swiss chard, among others.

incidental group

Fats and sugars are considered part of an incidental food group, since by eating foods from the three previous groups we obtain virtually all that is necessary for good nutrition. Among the fats are found: oil, butter, margarine, mayonnaise, and cream; and among the sugars: honey, sugar, sweets, jellies, and soft drinks, among others. Fats and sugars are high in calories, so experts recommend moderating our consumption of them to prevent the weight gain and obesity, which lead to other problems such as diabetes, hypertension, high levels of cholesterol and triglycerides in the blood, and heart disease.

a correct diet

Since ancient times the dinner table has been one of the pleasantest and most delightful places for families and friends to gather. And so it is still. This is no accident, since the agreeable smells and flavors of food, especially if it is presented in an appetizing way, lead to emotional satisfaction, which helps people live happily together.

From a biological point of view, an individual's diet should provide the nutrition necessary for the growth, development, and proper maintenance of an organism.

Nevertheless, in our eagerness to create delicious and attractive dishes, we often neglect the necessities and offer our guests only one of the basic food groups.

The pace of modern life demands high performance from every person in every area of involvement: in the workplace, in sports, in social life, and elsewhere. This is an excellent reason to eat right. A healthy diet possesses the following characteristics:

complete It should meet daily nutritional requirements. This can be accomplished by serving at least one food from each section of this book at breakfast, lunch, and dinner. For example: A lunch menu might include Aromatic Salad, Mediterranean Pasta, Citrus Salmon, and Fruit Crystal.

sufficient It ought to contain enough food to satisfy a person's appetite, meeting caloric requirements according to age, sex, height, metabolism, and physical activity.

balanced For any living thing to make the best use of them, the percentages of various nutrients it ingests ought to be in balance. The ideal proportion is: 50–60% carbohydrates, 15–20% proteins, and 25–30% lipids, or fats. Among the lipids are all fats of animal origin (found in red meat, cheese, milk, chicken, etc.).

varied It should include different foods and ways of preparing the dishes, making use of fruits and vegetables in season. For example: baked potatoes may be served on one day, mashed potatoes on another, and leek-and-potato soup on yet another.

hygienic For food to be healthful, it must not contain biological or chemical contaminants, microbes, or toxins. For example: wash vegetables and fruits well before eating them, and be sure to store them properly.

appropriate It ought to be adapted to each person according to age, state of health, habits, income, and the climate zone in which the person lives.

what to consider to achieve
a healthy and delicious menu

A healthy and delicious menu is one that offers good nutrition in appetizing dishes. In order to do this, keep in mind:

moderate use of fats. Limit the consumption of foods high in saturated fat and cholesterol, since these are high in calories and lead to health problems. Avoid breaded and fried food, thickened sauces, and animal fats (cream, butter, fatty cheeses, bacon, and salad dressings).

Cut back on the use of vegetable fats (vegetable oil, olive oil, and avocado oil). A suggestion: Replace cooking oil with cooking spray, or use an oil sprayer. Use alternative cooking methods such as roasting, baking, and steaming.

moderate use of salt. Avoid or reduce salt consumption, especially in people with a tendency toward fluid retention (edema) or with arterial hypertension. Suggestion: Herbs and spices that bring out the flavors and scents of foods can substitute for salt.

preferred meats. Eat turkey, chicken, fish, and veal, since they have less cholesterol.

preferred foods in season. Be aware of the variety available in your market, since these foods are freshest and most economical.

diversity of colors and textures. Include foods of varied colors and textures, since these help to make dishes more appetizing and attractive.

to **know and remember**

Healthy eating should be an everyday way of life, and it should include every member of the family. It should not be seen as a harsh dietary regimen or as the result of suffering a health problem. Every meal should be a treat for the eyes, the nose, and the palate.

Acquiring good eating habits is the best way to prevent health problems, to stay in good shape, and to feel satisfied after eating.

If you choose one recipe from each section of this book per meal, you will be planning a menu that provides you with a well-balanced diet. And you will enjoy the many delicious pleasures of light Latin cooking.

vegetables in season

january	february	march	april
Beets·Cabbage·Carrots· Cauliflower·Celery· Corn·Cucumber· Eggplant·Garlic· Green chiles·Lettuce·Onions· Radishes·Spinach·Squash· Swiss chard·Tomatoes.	Beets·Cabbage· Cauliflower·Celery·Corn· Cucumber·Eggplant· Garlic·Green beans· Green chiles·Lettuce·Onions· Peas·Potatoes·Prickly pear pads·Radishes·Spinach· Swiss chard·Tomatoes.	Cabbage·Carrots·Cauliflower· Celery·Chayote·Corn· Cucumber·Garlic· Green beans·Lettuce· Onions·Peas·Potatoes· Prickly pear pads·Radishes· Spinach·Squash· Swiss chard·Tomatoes.	Carrots·Cauliflower·Celery· Chayote·Corn· Cucumber·Garlic· Green beans·Lettuce· Onions·Peas·Prickly pear pads·Spinach·Squash· Swiss chard·Tomatoes.

may	june	july	august
Carrots·Cauliflower·Celery· Chayote·Corn·Cucumber· Garlic·Green beans·Green chiles·Lettuce·Onions· Peas·Prickly pear pads· Spinach·Squash· Swiss chard·Tomatoes· Watercress.	Carrots·Cauliflower·Celery· Chayote·Corn·Cucumber·Garlic· Green beans·Green Chiles· Greens·Lettuce·Onions·Peas· Prickly pear pads· Spinach·Squash·Swiss chard·Tomatoes· Watercress.	Cabbage·Carrots·Cauliflower· Celery·Chayote·Corn· Cucumber·Garlic·Green beans·Green chiles· Greens·Lettuce·Onions· Peas·Prickly pear pads· Squash·Swiss chard· Tomatoes.	Cabbage·Carrots· Cauliflower·Chayote· Corn·Cucumber· Green beans·Green chiles·Lettuce·Onions· Peas·Potatoes·Squash· Tomatillos·Tomatoes.

september	october	november	december
Cabbage·Carrots· Cauliflower·Corn· Cucumber·Eggplant· Green beans·Green chiles· Lettuce·Onions·Peas· Potatoes·Squash· Tomatillos·Tomatoes.	Cabbage·Carrots· Corn·Cucumber· Eggplant·Green beans· Green chiles·Lettuce· Potatoes·Squash· Tomatillos·Tomatoes.	Cabbage·Carrots· Green beans· Lettuce·Potatoes· Spinach· Squash· Tomatillos· Tomatoes.	Beets· Cabbage· Carrots· Lettuce· Spinach· Squash· Tomatoes.

Based on growing seasons in Mexico. Choose fresh local produce wherever you are.

fruits in season

january	february	march	april
Avocados·Bananas· Cherimoya·Coconut· Grapefruit·Guava·Jicama· Lemons·Limes·Oranges· Papaya·Pineapple· Pomegranates·Sapodilla· Strawberries·Sugarcane· Tamarind·Tangerines.	Avocados·Bananas· Cantaloupe·Cherimoya· Coconut·Grapefruit·Guava· Lemons·Oranges·Papaya· Pineapple·Pomegranates· Soursop·Strawberries· Tamarind·Tangerines.	Avocados·Bananas· Cantaloupe·Coconut· Grapefruit·Lemons· Mamey·Mango· Oranges·Papaya· Pineapple·Soursop· Strawberries· Tamarind·Watermelon.	Bananas·Cantaloupe· Grapefruit·Kiwi· Lemons·Mamey· Mango·Oranges· Papaya·Pineapple· Soursop·Strawberries· Tamarind·Watermelon.

may	june	july	august
Apricots·Bananas· Cantaloupe· Figs·Kiwi· Lemons·Mamey· Mango·Papaya· Pears·Pineapple· Plums·Watermelon.	Apricots·Bananas· Cantaloupe· Figs·Grapes·Kiwi· Lemons·Mamey·Mango· Papaya·Passion fruit· Peaches·Pears·Pineapple· Plums·Pomegranates· Watermelon.	Apples·Apricots· Bananas·Cantaloupe· Cherries·Figs·Grapes· Lemons·Papaya· Passion fruit·Peaches·Pears· Pineapple·Plums· Pomegranates·Prickly pears· Quince·Watermelon.	Apples·Apricots· Bananas·Cantaloupe· Cherries·Figs·Grapes· Guava·Lemons·Papaya· Passion fruit·Peaches· Pears·Plums·Pomegranates· Prickly pears·Quince· Watermelon.

september	october	november	december
Apples·Apricots· Bananas·Cantaloupe· Cherries·Grapes·Grapefruit· Guava·Lemons·Limes· Papaya·Passion fruit·Peaches· Pears·Plums·Pomegranates· Prickly pears· Quince·Watermelon.	Apples·Avocados· Bananas·Cherimoya·Dates· Grapefruit·Guava·Lemons· Limes·Oranges· Papaya·Passion fruit·Pears· Prickly pears·Sapodilla· Tangerines.	Avocados·Bananas· Cherimoya·Dates·Grapefruit· Guava·Jicama·Lemons· Limes·Oranges·Papaya· Pomegranates· Prickly pears·Sapodilla· Sugarcane· Tangerines.	Avocados·Bananas· Cherimoya·Dates·Grapefruit· Guava·Jicama·Lemons· Limes·Oranges·Papaya· Pomegranates· Prickly pears·Sapodilla· Sugarcane·Strawberries· Tamarind·Tangerines.

Based on growing seasons in Mexico. Choose fresh local produce wherever you are.

suggestions for **preparing and cooking**

vegetable	preparation	boil	steam
artichokes	Cut off the tips of the external leaves and of the stem. Rub with lemon juice to prevent discoloration.	30 to 40 minutes or until the leaves separate easily	45 minutes or until fork-tender
asparagus	Trim away the tough ends.	8 to 10 minutes	15 minutes
beets	Trim slightly.	30 to 40 minutes	12 to 30 minutes
broccoli	Divide into florets, trim off the tough stem.	5 to 10 minutes	10 to 15 minutes
carrots	Trim the ends and peel.	15 to 20 minutes	20 to 25 minutes
celery	Separate stalks, removing strings if needed.	5 minutes	10 to 15 minutes
eggplant	Peel, salt, let stand 30 minutes, and rinse.	5 to 10 minutes	10 to 15 minutes
fennel	Remove roots and outer leaves.	10 to 15 minutes	5 to 20 minutes
green beans	Snap off the tips and remove any string.	30 to 40 minutes	15 minutes
leeks	Cut off root end.	10 to 15 minutes	15 to 20 minutes
mushrooms	Trim.	5 to 10 minutes	——
potatoes	Peel.	15 to 20 minutes	25 to 30 minutes
spinach	Trim roots and tough stems.	5 to 10 minutes	10 to 15 minutes
zucchini	Trim ends.	5 to 10 minutes	5 to 10 minutes

Cooking times are approximate and may vary with different elevations.

in english and spanish

Bean: frijol: poroto: caraota

Bean sprout: frijol de soya: brote de soya: germinado de soya

Beet: betabel: remolacha

Blackberry: zarzamora: mora

Blueberry: mora azul

Celery: apio

Corn (fresh): elote: choclo: jojoto

Leek: poro: puerro

Lemongrass: limoncillo: hierba Luisa

Pearl onion: cebollita de Cambray: cebolla de verdeo

Pepper, chile: pimiento: pimentón: ají

Pineapple: piña: ananá

Shallot: chalote: echalote

Snow pea: chícharo chino: vainita china: chaucha china

Squash, zucchini: calabacín: calabacita

Strawberry: fresa, frutilla

Sweet potato: camote: batata

Tomato: jitomate: tomate

recipes and secrets...

fish, chicken, and meat

vegetables
and more

things to consider before **preparing a salad**

Wash the vegetables under running water.
Dry the vegetables in a salad spinner.
Tear the leaves by hand; a knife blade may discolor them.
To store salad materials, wrap them in paper towels, place
them in a plastic bag, and refrigerate.

vegetables and more

little secrets

To concentrate the flavor of salad dressings, we recommend refrigerating them for two hours before serving.

To blend salad dressings effectively, it's best to add the oil last.

To wash mushrooms, it's better to hold them under running water, since if they are submerged they will become soggy.

To remove the bitter flavor from eggplant, slice it, sprinkle it with salt, let it drain in a colander for half an hour, and rinse it before using.

To cook vegetables, it is important to submerge them in water that is already boiling.

To plan a menu, it's important to use vegetables and fruits in season, since they are fresher and more economical.

portobello mushroom salad

Serves 4

ingredients

oil in a spray bottle
4 large portobello mushrooms or 8 smaller ones
12 cherry tomatoes

dressing

3 tomatoes, seeded and cut into cubes
$1/2$ cup orange juice
6 tablespoons balsamic vinegar
$1/2$ teaspoon crushed garlic
2 tablespoons olive oil
finely chopped basil
salt and pepper

preparation

Mix the ingredients of the dressing.
Spray a skillet with oil, and sauté the mushrooms.
Remove from the pan.
Pour the dressing over the mushrooms, and decorate with the cherry tomatoes.

little secret · Serve hot or cold.

original green salad

Serves 6

ingredients

1 large or 2 small heads romaine lettuce
1 large or 2 small heads escarole
2 cups arugula leaves
1 cup dried tomatoes, rehydrated for 8 hours
in 1 cup orange juice with
2 tablespoons olive oil
18 cherry tomatoes

dressing

1 teaspoon honey
1 teaspoon mashed garlic
1 teaspoon finely chopped or grated ginger
1 tablespoon soy sauce
1 tablespoon Dijon mustard
1 tablespoon lemon juice
2 tablespoons balsamic vinegar
1 tablespoon orange juice
2 tablespoons oil
salt and pepper

preparation

Mix the ingredients of the dressing.
Pour the dressing over the vegetables, remembering first
to strain the rehydrated tomatoes.

little secret Serve the salad with strips of toasted pita bread.

aromatic salad

Serves 4

ingredients

1 pound raw white mushrooms, sliced
2 stalks raw fennel, thinly sliced
2 raw artichoke hearts, thinly sliced
20 very thin slices Parmesan cheese

dressing

$^1/_2$ cup rice vinegar
$^1/_4$ cup lemon juice
$^1/_4$ cup olive oil
4 teaspoons basil, fresh or dried
salt and pepper

preparation

Mix the ingredients of the dressing.
Pour the dressing over the vegetables, and garnish
with the cheese slices.

little secrets

Cider vinegar can replace the rice vinegar.
Sprinkle the sliced mushrooms, fennel, and artichoke hearts with
lemon juice to keep them from discoloring.

greens with **mango dressing**

Serves 2

ingredients

3 cups salad greens (see "little secret" below)
$^1/_2$ cup alfalfa sprouts
$^1/_2$ cup bean sprouts

dressing

1 tablespoon lemon juice
2 tablespoons orange juice
$^3/_4$ tablespoon Dijon mustard
1 tablespoon oil
1 teaspoon chopped fresh cilantro
$^1/_2$ mango, cut into cubes

preparation

Purée together the ingredients of the dressing.
Pour the dressing over the vegetables.

little secret

This dressing is ideal with slightly bitter vegetables. You may use greens such as arugula, curly endive, Belgian endive, radicchio, purslane, etc.

fresh salad

Serves 6

ingredients

4 carrots, cut into sticks
2 small jicamas, cut into sticks
2 cucumbers, cut into sticks
1 cooked beet, cut into sticks

dressing

1 cup plain yogurt
$^1/_2$ cup orange juice
2 tablespoons mayonnaise
$^1/_2$ teaspoon mashed garlic
1 teaspoon dry thyme
salt and pepper

preparation

Mix the ingredients of the dressing.
Pour the dressing over the vegetables.

little secret : You can substitute celery for jicama.

squash blossom salad

Serves 6

ingredients

1 large or 2 small heads escarole
1 large or 2 small heads romaine lettuce
3 zucchini, julienned
1 pound zucchini blossoms or other squash blossoms
4 ounces crumbled goat cheese
salt

dressing

$^1/_2$ cup white wine vinegar
$^1/_2$ cup orange juice
1 tablespoon chicken bouillon powder
3 tablespoons shelled and toasted pumpkin seeds
1 small clove garlic
2 teaspoons honey
2 teaspoons olive oil
pepper

preparation

Purée the dressing ingredients together.
Pour the dressing over the vegetables.
Add the goat cheese.
Correct for salt.

salad of **belgian endive and...**

Serves 6

ingredients

4 Belgian endives, leaves separated, hearts reserved
2 pounds asparagus, cooked al dente
2 beets, cooked and julienned
1 large or 2 small heads escarole, leaves separated

dressing

$^1/_2$ cup orange juice
2 teaspoons honey
1 teaspoon Dijon mustard
6 tablespoons tarragon vinegar
3 tablespoons olive oil
2 tablespoons corn oil
salt and pepper

preparation

Mix the dressing ingredients.
Arrange the endive leaves in a circle on a platter. Place the asparagus spears and beet strips on top of the endive leaves, pile the escarole in the center, and top with the endive hearts.
Pour the dressing over the vegetables.

green bean and squash salad

Serves 6

ingredients

1 pound green beans
2 pinches of baking soda, divided
2 pinches of salt, divided
1 pound round summer squash or zucchini,
cut into thick wedges
6 cherry tomatoes
$^1/_2$ red onion, cut in slices

dressing

6 tablespoons red wine vinegar
1 tablespoon Dijon mustard
$1^1/_2$ teaspoons sugar
5 tablespoons olive oil
1 tablespoon very finely chopped parsley
1 tablespoon finely chopped red onion
salt and pepper

preparation

Mix the dressing ingredients.
Cook the green beans in boiling water with one pinch each of baking soda and salt for 7 minutes.
Cook the squash for 5 minutes using the same method.
Pour the dressing over the vegetables, both raw and cooked. Serve cold.

roasted vegetables

Serves 6

ingredients

10 baby potatoes, cut in half and parboiled
1 pound baby carrots, parboiled
1 eggplant, peeled and diced
1 red bell pepper, seeded and diced
1 yellow bell pepper, seeded and diced
1 green bell pepper, seeded and diced
1 onion, diced
4 zucchini, julienned
$1/_2$ cup broccoli florets
2 cups white mushrooms
1 cup snow peas
1 cup julienned portobello, oyster, shiitake, or other mushrooms
4 medium tomatoes, diced
$1/_4$ cup olive oil
2 teaspoons tarragon, fresh or dried
salt

vinaigrette

1 tablespoon Dijon mustard
6 tablespoons rice vinegar
3 tablespoons olive oil
$1^1/_2$ tablespoons teriyaki sauce
2 cloves garlic, mashed
3 tablespoons chopped parsley
salt and pepper

preparation

Place all the vegetables in a large bowl.
Marinate them with the oil, tarragon, and salt for 20 minutes.
Remove the vegetables from the bowl, drain, and place in a baking dish.
Bake at 350 degrees F for 40 to 45 minutes, stirring occasionally.
Serve the vegetables at room temperature on a platter.
Pass the vinaigrette separately.

little secret   Try cider vinegar instead of rice vinegar.

oriental vegetables

Serves 4

ingredients

2 cups bean sprouts
4 cups snow peas, parboiled
2 cups halved mushrooms
2 cups julienned celery
2 cups julienned jicama
2 tablespoons finely chopped green onion
soy sauce to taste

preparation

Spray a skillet with oil, and sauté all the vegetables except the green onion for 5 minutes, stirring occasionally.
Sprinkle with the chopped onion and soy sauce.
Serve immediately.

little secrets

The vegetables should stay crunchy.
The jicama can be replaced with raw turnip.

vegetarian kabobs

Serves 2

ingredients

oil in a spray bottle
1 eggplant, cut into cubes
2 large zucchini, cut into cubes
$1/_2$ red bell pepper, cut into squares
$1/_2$ yellow bell pepper, cut into squares
4 cooked baby potatoes
4 broccoli florets, parboiled
4 cherry tomatoes
salt
4 skewers

dressing

6 tablespoons balsamic vinegar
2 tablespoons finely chopped red onion
1 tablespoon honey
2 tablespoons olive oil
salt and pepper

preparation

Mix together the dressing ingredients.
Spray a skillet with oil and cook the vegetables one by one,
adding salt to taste.
Place the cooked vegetables on the skewers.
Pour the vinaigrette dressing over the kabobs.

vegetables baked in foil

Serves 6

ingredients

3 potatoes, peeled and julienned
3 carrots, peeled and julienned
3 zucchini, julienned
1 cup snow peas
3 turnips, peeled and julienned
1 cup julienned oyster, shiitake, or portobello mushrooms
6 slices fresh ginger, finely chopped
salt and pepper
6 tablespoons soy sauce or tamarind sauce
6 squares aluminum foil, 12 x 12 inches each

preparation

Distribute on each foil square an equal quantity of each vegetable and chopped ginger.
Season each portion with salt, pepper, and 1 tablespoon soy or tamarind sauce.
Fold the foil into 6 sealed packets.
Bake at 350 degrees F for 35 minutes.
Serve the vegetables in their packets to best enjoy their juices and aroma.

vegetable fiesta with eggplant purée

Serves 4

ingredients

oil in a spray bottle
1$\frac{1}{2}$ medium eggplants, unpeeled, diced
3 small zucchini, diced
1 red bell pepper, julienned
$\frac{1}{2}$ green bell pepper, julienned
1$\frac{1}{2}$ onions, in thin lengthwise slices
3 large cloves garlic, mashed
4 ripe tomatoes, blanched, peeled, seeded, and diced
fresh thyme, basil, and rosemary
salt and pepper

eggplant purée

oil in a spray bottle
2 medium eggplants
4 cloves garlic
fresh basil
2 anchovies
salt and pepper

preparation

Spray a skillet with oil, and brown separately the eggplant, zucchini, bell pepper, and onion. Reserve.
Spray another skillet with oil, sauté the garlic, add the tomatoes, and cook over moderate heat for 15 minutes.
Add water if necessary. Finally, add the browned vegetables, fresh herbs, and salt and pepper.
Simmer until the liquid is reduced but not dry.
Prepare the eggplant purée.
Line each of 4 molds with a shallow layer of eggplant purée, then fill them with the cooked vegetables.
Unmold for serving.

eggplant purée

Spray the whole eggplants with oil, and bake at 350 degrees F for 1 hour. Once they are tender, remove peels.
Spray another skillet with oil and sauté the garlic, adding the eggplant (cut into quarters), basil, anchovies, and salt and pepper, and let cook for 10 minutes.
Purée all the ingredients together.

little secret · Try this either cold or hot.

vegetable spiral

Serves 8

ingredients

oil in a spray bottle
1 large eggplant, sliced lengthwise into 8 thin slices
2 zucchini, julienned
1 onion, thinly sliced
2 tomatoes, thinly sliced
salt and pepper
oregano
4 ounces queso panela (or other white cheese—see "little secret" below), cut into 8 rectangles

tomato sauce as an accompaniment

preparation

Spray a skillet with oil, and brown each type of vegetable separately.

Stack the vegetables one on top of another in 8 piles, beginning with the eggplant, followed by the zucchini, the onion, and the tomato.

Season with salt, pepper, and oregano.

Place a slice of cheese on the top of each stack, roll it up in the eggplant slice, and secure it with a toothpick.

Bake at 350 degrees F for 10 minutes.

Serve hot, accompanied with tomato sauce.

little secret

Good substitutes for queso panela include any mild white cheese, such as Monterey Jack, Muenster, mozzarella, or mild goat cheese.

broccoli purée

Serves 4

ingredients

1 pound broccoli florets (without thick stems)
2 tablespoons olive oil
salt

preparation

Blanch the broccoli for 3 minutes in a large pot of boiling water, drain, and reserve $1/2$ cup of the water.
Purée the hot broccoli in a food processor with the reserved water, olive oil, and salt, or pass all ingredients through a food mill, until it reaches a fairly smooth consistency.

carrots tahi

Serves 2

ingredients

1 pound baby carrots, peeled and cooked

tahi sauce

4 teaspoons cornstarch
1 teaspoon finely grated fresh ginger
3 tablespoons brown sugar
1 cup orange juice

preparation

Mix the ingredients of the tahi sauce and pour it into a skillet. Simmer over low heat, stirring constantly, until the sauce is blended and thickened.
Add the carrots to the tahi sauce, and simmer for 5 more minutes.
Serve hot.

pastas,
potatoes, and rice

vegetable rolls

Serves 3

ingredients

oil in a spray bottle
$1/2$ medium onion, diced
1 shallot, chopped
$1/4$ red bell pepper, diced
$1/4$ green bell pepper, diced
1 chayote, diced
$1/2$ eggplant, diced
3 zucchini, diced
2 peeled and seeded tomatoes, cubed
oregano
salt and pepper
3 rounds pita bread, each split in half
6 ounces crumbled goat cheese
pink peppercorns for decoration (optional)

preparation

Spray a skillet with oil, and sauté the onion, shallot, and red and green peppers. Then add the chayote and eggplant. In 5 minutes add the zucchini, tomato, and oregano. Add salt and pepper. Add water as needed to prevent the mixture from drying out.

Distribute the cooked vegetables over each piece of pita bread, then add the goat cheese.

Roll the pieces of pita bread to form vegetable rolls.

Bake at 350 degrees F for 10 minutes.

tricolor fusilli with pepper sauce

Serves 2

ingredients

oil in a spray bottle
$1^1/_2$ red bell peppers
2 slices leek
2 cloves garlic
2 cups chicken broth
7 ounces tricolor fusilli pasta, cooked al dente
2 tablespoons grated Parmesan cheese

preparation

To make the sauce, spray a skillet with oil, and add the peppers, skin side up, each cut into 4 pieces, and the slices of leek. Sauté for 10 minutes, then add the garlic cloves and sauté them.

Finally, add the broth and simmer for 15 minutes. Allow to cool, purée, and strain.

Put the hot fusilli on serving plates, pour the sauce over the pasta, and sprinkle it with Parmesan cheese.

noodles with rosy sauce

Serves 4

ingredients

oil in a spray bottle
$^1/_2$ onion, finely diced
1 clove garlic, mashed
2 ripe tomatoes, peeled, seeded, and finely diced
1 fresh bay leaf
1 sprig fresh thyme
1 sprig fresh celery leaves (from 1 rib)
3 or 4 fresh basil leaves
2 cups chopped marinated artichoke hearts
(reserve 2 tablespoons marinade)
1 jar pimientos, cut into thin strips
20 black olives, pitted
2 tablespoons tomato purée
salt and pepper
2 ounces goat cheese
14 ounces flat pasta (linguine, fettuccine, egg
noodles), cooked al dente

preparation

Spray a skillet with oil.
Sauté the onion and garlic with the tomatoes, then add
the fresh herbs.
Finally, mix in the artichoke hearts, marinade, pimientos,
olives, tomato purée, and enough water to keep everything
moist. Season with salt and pepper.
Remove the herbs. Add the crumbled goat cheese.
Mix the sauce with the noodles.

mediterranean pasta salad

Serves 4

ingredients

7 ounces penne pasta, cooked al dente and
cooled
8 ounces cherry tomatoes, cut in quarters
4 ounces goat cheese, crumbled
20 black olives
basil, finely chopped

dressing

3 tablespoons balsamic vinegar
2 tablespoons olive oil
$1^1/_2$ tablespoons water
pinch of sugar
salt and pepper

preparation

Mix the cold pasta with the tomatoes, goat cheese, olives,
and basil.
Mix the ingredients of the dressing.
Pour the dressing over the pasta.

spaghetti al pesto

Serves 2

ingredients

1 cup finely chopped basil
1 small shallot, finely chopped
13 ounces soft tofu, crumbled
12 walnuts, finely chopped
2 tablespoons low-salt soy sauce
2 tablespoons olive oil
7 ounces spaghetti, cooked al dente

preparation

To make the pesto, use a mortar and pestle (or a blender or food processor) to grind together the basil and the shallot.
Add the tofu, nuts, soy sauce, and olive oil to make a sauce.
Place the hot pasta on plates, and top it with room-temperature pesto.

little secret

You may replace the tofu with ricotta cheese.

cannelloni stuffed with spinach

Serves 2

ingredients

oil in a spray bottle
$^1/_2$ red onion, finely chopped
1 cup cooked spinach, chopped and squeezed dry
$^1/_2$ cup finely chopped mushrooms
$1^1/_2$ cups ricotta cheese
$^1/_2$ cup grated Parmesan cheese
1 egg
$^1/_8$ teaspoon nutmeg
salt and pepper
4 pieces fresh cannelloni pasta or 7 ounces
manicotti or large shells, cooked al dente (or
substitute no-boil lasagna pasta, softened in
hot water)

tomato sauce

2 well-ripened tomatoes
1 clove garlic, peeled
fresh basil, thyme, and rosemary
salt and pepper

preparation

To prepare the sauce, plunge the tomatoes into boiling water, peel and seed them, and dice the pulp. Spray a skillet with oil, and add the garlic. Let it brown lightly, then blend in the tomatoes and finally the herbs. Season with salt and pepper, and add enough water to keep the sauce moist. Simmer for 15 minutes, and remove the garlic.

To make the filling, spray a skillet with oil, add the onion, spinach, and mushrooms, and cook together briefly. In a mixing bowl, stir together the cheeses, egg, spinach mixture, and nutmeg until they are completely blended. Season with salt and pepper.

Fill the cannelloni with the spinach mixture. Pour half the sauce into a baking dish, arrange the stuffed pasta on top, and cover with the remaining sauce.

Bake at 350 degrees F for 20 minutes. Serve immediately.

mashed sweet potatoes

Serves 6

ingredients

3 sweet potatoes, cooked
2 white potatoes, cooked
oil in a spray bottle
1 onion, sliced in wedges
1 clove garlic, mashed
$^1/_2$ cup chicken broth
salt
1 tablespoon ground ginger
1 tablespoon curry powder

preparation

Purée the hot sweet and white potatoes together.
Spray a skillet with oil, and sauté the onion and the garlic.
Then purée them together with the chicken broth in a blender. Stir this mixture into the potato purée.
Heat, seasoning with the salt and the spices.

mashed potatoes with **dill**

Serves 6

ingredients

6 medium potatoes, cooked and peeled
$^1/_2$ cup chicken broth
2 tablespoons dill weed, either dry or
minced fresh
salt and pepper
oil in a spray bottle
12 very thin potato slices, parboiled

preparation

Purée the whole potatoes with the chicken broth, and add
the dill. Season with salt and pepper and reserve.
Spray an ovenproof casserole dish with oil, line it with the
potato slices, and spread the mashed potatoes on top.
Bake at 350 degrees F for 10 minutes.

mashed potatoes and **carrots**

Serves 6

ingredients

oil in a spray bottle
1 cup finely chopped leek
6 carrots, cooked (reserve some of the water)
6 medium potatoes, cooked
salt and pepper

preparation

Spray a skillet with oil, and sauté the leek.
Make a purée of the hot carrots and potatoes, adding a little of
the water in which you boiled them.
Mix the purée with the leek, and allow it to heat briefly. Season
with salt and pepper.

potatoes stuffed with spinach

Serves 2

ingredients

2 cooked potatoes
2 cups cooked spinach
1 egg white
1 teaspoon finely chopped onion
2 teaspoons grated Parmesan cheese
salt and pepper

preparation

Scoop out the insides of the potatoes, reserving the contents of one of them for this recipe. Add salt to each potato shell.

Purée the spinach, egg white, onion, and reserved potato flesh. Season with salt and pepper.

Stuff each potato with the spinach mixture, and top with the grated Parmesan.

Bake at 350 degrees F until the cheese is lightly browned.

tiny new potatoes **with herbs**

Serves 4

ingredients

1 pound tiny new potatoes
oil in a spray bottle
2 tablespoons olive oil
1 teaspoon grated lemon zest
1 tablespoon chopped fresh basil
1 tablespoon chopped fresh parsley
salt and pepper
1 teaspoon lemon juice

preparation

Place the potatoes, unpeeled, in a saucepan.
Add water to cover, and bring them to a boil on high heat.
Cover them, reduce the heat, and cook them until they are barely tender, approximately 10 minutes.
Drain the potatoes.
Spray a skillet with oil, add the olive oil, lemon zest, basil, parsley, and potatoes. Season with salt and pepper.
Cook on low heat, mixing these ingredients.
Add the lemon juice, stir, and serve immediately.

brown rice **with mushrooms**

Serves 4

ingredients

oil in a spray bottle
2 tablespoons finely chopped shallots
2 tablespoons finely chopped onion
1 cup brown rice
3$\frac{1}{2}$ cups water
salt
2 tablespoons finely chopped chives
3 cups halved mushrooms

preparation

Spray a saucepan with oil, and sauté the shallots, onion, and brown rice.
Add the water and salt. Allow the mixture to come to a boil, lower the heat, stir in the chives, cover the pan, and simmer until the rice is tender, about 45 minutes.
Spray a skillet with oil and brown the mushrooms. Add the salt. Before removing the rice from the pan, stir in the mushrooms.

little secrets

Brown rice cooks more quickly when it has been soaked overnight.
You can use various kinds of mushrooms.

green rice

Serves 2

ingredients

oil in a spray bottle
1 tablespoon finely chopped shallot (or garlic)
1 tablespoon chopped onion
$1^1/_2$ cups rice
$^1/_2$ cup cooked, puréed spinach
3 cups water
salt

preparation

Spray a saucepan with oil, and sauté the shallot
and onion.
Blend in the rice and sauté for a few moments.
Add the spinach.
Pour in the water and salt. When it reaches a boil, lower
the heat and cover the pot. Simmer for 20 minutes.

yellow rice

Serves 2

ingredients

oil in a spray bottle
2 slices leek
1 garlic clove, quartered
$^1/_4$ teaspoon saffron soaked in 2 tablespoons
cold water for 10 minutes
$^1/_2$ cup rice
1 cup water
salt

preparation

Spray a saucepan with oil, and sauté the leek and garlic.
Then purée them with the saffron and its soaking water.
Pour this purée into a saucepan sprayed with oil, stir in the
rice, and sauté for a few moments.
Add the water and the salt. When it reaches a boil, lower the
heat and cover the pot. Simmer for 20 minutes.

rice with **guajillo chile**

Serves 2

ingredients

1 clove garlic, finely chopped
2 tablespoons guajillo chile that has been
seeded, toasted, and puréed with a little water,
or 2 tablespoons guajillo powder or any other
spicy, dynamic chile powder
2 tablespoons chopped onion
oil in a spray bottle
$1/2$ cup rice
$1\ 1/2$ cups water
salt

preparation

Purée the garlic, chile, and onion.
Spray a saucepan with oil, and add and gently cook the
purée.
Add the rice, cook a few moments, and stir in the water and
salt. When it reaches a boil, lower the heat and cover the
pot. Simmer for 20 minutes.

little secret · The guajillo chile can be replaced with red bell pepper.

eggplant stuffed with rice

Serves 2

ingredients

2 large eggplants, not peeled, cut in half and
soaked in salted water for 30 minutes
salt
oil in a spray bottle
1 teaspoon mashed garlic
1 teaspoon chopped red onion
$^3/_4$ cup peeled, seeded, and diced tomatoes
$^1/_2$ cup rice
2 cups water
oregano
2 tablespoons Parmesan cheese

preparation

Remove the eggplant from the water, and scoop out the
inside. Save a little of the inside of the eggplant, and salt it.
Bake the eggplant shell at 350 degrees F for 15 minutes.
Dice the reserved eggplant.
Spray a frying pan with oil, and sauté the garlic, onion,
tomato, and diced eggplant.
Add the rice, allowing it to sauté briefly. Add the water, salt,
and oregano. Lower the heat, cover, and simmer until the
rice is tender.
Stuff the eggplants with the cooked rice mixture. Sprinkle
with Parmesan cheese.
Bake at 350 degrees F for 15 minutes longer.

rice **tabouli**

Serves 4

ingredients

1 cup wild rice, or a mix of wild and white
rices (to be cooked separately)
2 cups water
salt

dressing

2 tablespoons olive oil
3 tablespoons balsamic vinegar
1 tablespoon lemon juice
$1/4$ cup Worcestershire sauce
salt and pepper

salad

2 tomatoes, quartered
1 cucumber, peeled, seeded, and diced
$1/3$ cup finely chopped fresh mint
$1/3$ cup finely chopped fresh basil
2 tablespoons finely chopped fresh chives
black olives

preparation

Cook the rice (or cook the two types of rice separately) and
let it cool.
Mix the ingredients of the dressing.
Mix the salad ingredients with the rice to make the tabouli.
Pour the dressing over the tabouli.

little secret

Try serving this in "bowls" made of large curved lettuce
leaves.

vegetarian paella

Serves 4

ingredients

oil in a spray bottle
2 tablespoons thinly sliced leek
3 tablespoons thinly sliced red onion
1 teaspoon mashed garlic
$1/_2$ green bell pepper, julienned
$1/_2$ yellow bell pepper, julienned
1 cup diced eggplant, with peel
1 cup peeled, seeded, and diced tomato
$1^1/_2$ cups rice
$1/_2$ cup dry white wine
3 cups water
salt
1 cup baby corn
1 cup thinly sliced mushrooms
oregano, basil, and parsley, finely chopped

preparation

Spray a large skillet with oil, and add the leek, onion, garlic, peppers, eggplant, and tomato. When they are golden, add the rice and sauté for a few moments.
Pour in the wine, and leave uncovered to evaporate the alcohol.
Add the water, salt, baby corn, and mushrooms. When it comes to a boil, lower the heat, cover the pan, and simmer until the rice is done (approximately 20 minutes). Before serving, add the herbs and mix well.

fish,
chicken,
and meat

fish, chicken, and meat

*little
secrets*

When you select fish, remember:

Its flesh should be firm and smooth, never flabby or soft.

The gills should be red and shiny, without grayish marks.

The skin should be shiny and moist.

The eyes should be shiny, bulging, and moist.

The aroma should be fresh and pleasant.

When you select poultry, remember:

The meat should be well formed and unmarked, even if frozen.

The skin should appear moist but not soggy.

Feed can affect the color of the skin and the flavor of the meat.

When you select veal, remember:

The color of the meat should be rosy with no spots or grayish tone.

Its aroma should be faint and almost imperceptible.

citrus salmon

Serves 2

ingredients

$^2/_3$ cup orange juice
$^1/_3$ cup orange marmalade
$1^1/_2$ teaspoons brown sugar
2 tablespoons finely chopped onion
1 teaspoon grated fresh ginger
12 ounces fresh salmon
salt and pepper
2 tablespoons finely chopped cilantro

preparation

Blend together the juice, marmalade, sugar, onion, and ginger.
Place the salmon, already salted and peppered, skin-side-down in a baking dish.
Pour the mixture over the salmon.
Cover and refrigerate for one hour.
Bake uncovered at 350 degrees F for 20 minutes. Garnish with cilantro before serving.

little secrets

Perfectly cooked salmon has a firm, juicy texture and a tender pink color.
You may use parsley in place of the cilantro.
Try decorating the salmon with orange peel, first blanched in hot water and cut into julienne matchsticks.

ginger salmon

Serves 6

ingredients

$^1/_2$ cup low-salt soy sauce
3 tablespoons rice vinegar
2 tablespoons oil
1 clove garlic, crushed
2 tablespoons finely chopped shallots
2 tablespoons finely chopped chives
2 tablespoons finely chopped fresh ginger
1 cup water
$2^1/_2$ pounds fresh salmon with skin
salt

preparation

Mix the soy sauce, vinegar, oil, garlic, shallot, chives, ginger, and water.
Place the salmon with the skin side down in a baking dish, pour the soy mixture over it, and refrigerate covered for one hour. **Add** salt if needed.
Bake uncovered at 350 degrees F for 25 minutes.

little secret · Cider vinegar can substitute for rice vinegar.

fish poached in **citrus broth**

Serves 6

ingredients

oil in a spray bottle
4 cloves garlic
1 leek, cut into thin crosswise slices, then cut
through the rings so they open up
$1/2$ onion, cut into thin wedges
1 red bell pepper, cut into julienne matchsticks
4 sprigs celery leaves
$2^1/_2$ pounds sea bass or red snapper, cut into 6
skinless portions
salt
1 cup water
several sprigs each cilantro and lemongrass
$1/2$ cup orange juice
$1/4$ cup lemon juice

preparation

Spray a large skillet with oil, and sauté the garlic, leek, onion, pepper, and celery leaves.

Add the fish and salt, and cover the pan. When the lower part of the fish changes color, add the water, and, once it comes to a boil, add cilantro and lemongrass.

Without turning the fish, poach uncovered for 10 more minutes, then flavor it with the orange and lemon juices.

fish in **parsley sauce**

Serves 4

ingredients

2 pounds red snapper in thick fillets
$1/4$ cup lemon juice
salt
oil in a spray bottle

sauce

2 cups parsley
$1/4$ cup lemon juice
2 tablespoons water
2 tablespoons Dijon mustard
2 tablespoons finely chopped onion
1 clove garlic
salt

preparation

Marinate the fish with the lemon juice and salt for 10 minutes.
Purée the sauce ingredients together.
Drain the fish.
Spray a baking dish with oil, add the fish, and pour the sauce on top.
Bake at 350 degrees F for 20 minutes.

fish "hamburgers"

Serves 2

ingredients

10 ounces firm-textured white fish, such as
grouper, snook, or fresh cod
1 tablespoon grated carrot
1 tablespoon minced onion
1 teaspoon chopped cilantro
pinch of saffron
1 teaspoon grated lemon zest
1 teaspoon pressed garlic
2 teaspoons fresh grated ginger
salt
1 egg white
oil in a spray bottle

preparation

Simmer the fish for 5 minutes, then grind or finely chop it.

Mix together the rest of the ingredients, finishing with the egg white, which should be lightly beaten before being mixed in.

Form into patties.

Spray a baking dish with oil, place the patties in the dish, and bake at 350 degrees F until they are browned.

little secrets

- If you don't have cilantro, use parsley.
- Try serving these with tomato sauce.

turkey breast with pearl onions and grapes

Serves 4

ingredients

oil in a spray bottle
3 pounds turkey breast, with bone
salt and pepper
2 cups pearl onions, peeled
1 tablespoon sugar
3 tablespoons balsamic vinegar
1 cup white wine
1 cup chicken broth
4 sprigs fresh marjoram (or 1 teaspoon dried)
2 bay leaves
1 pound green grapes

preparation

Spray a skillet with oil, and brown the turkey breast. Season it with salt and pepper.

Add the pearl onions and the sugar. Stir in the vinegar and the white wine.

Cook a few minutes to evaporate the alcohol. Finally, stir in the chicken broth, marjoram, and bay leaves, and cook for 5 more minutes.

Move everything to a baking dish, and bake at 350 degrees F until the turkey is brown and tender.

Add the grapes in the last 5 minutes, just to heat them through.

turkey breast with orange and oregano

Serves 4

ingredients

oil in a spray bottle
$1/_2$ turkey breast, with bone
salt and pepper
$1^1/_2$ cups orange juice
$1/_2$ cup white wine
oregano

preparation

Spray a skillet with oil, and brown the turkey breast. Season it with salt and pepper.
Mix the orange juice, white wine, and oregano.
Move the turkey to a baking dish, and add half of the juice mixture.
Bake at 350 degrees F until the turkey is brown, basting with the remaining juice to keep the meat from drying out.

chicken **in a veil**

Serves 6

ingredients

6 maguey leaves (see "little secrets" below)
6 boneless chicken-breast halves
salt and pepper
2 roasted ancho chiles (see "little secrets" below)
2 cloves garlic
6 pearl onions
$^1/_2$ cup water
oil in a spray bottle
6 tender prickly pear pads, cut into julienne matchsticks (see "little secrets" below)

preparation

Soak the maguey leaves (if using) in hot water until they become flexible.

Season the chicken breasts with salt and pepper.

Purée the chiles, garlic, and onions with the water. Spray a skillet with oil, add the purée, cook at moderate heat for a few minutes, and add salt and pepper. Do not let it dry out.

Cut each maguey leaf in half lengthwise, arrange the halves in the shape of a cross, place a chicken breast in the middle, top with sauce, and add the sliced prickly pear pads. So that no juice escapes, seal tightly, and tie the package with a long fiber from the maguey leaf, if you have it.

Bake at 350 degrees F for 30 minutes, or steam for the same amount of time.

little secrets

· Twelve-inch squares of aluminum foil or parchment paper can replace the maguey leaves.
· You may also use red bell peppers instead of ancho chiles, and green beans instead of prickly pear pads.

chicken flavored with **banana leaves**

Serves 4

ingredients

2 pounds whole squash blossoms
4 roasted poblano chiles, peeled, seeded, and cut into julienne matchsticks (wear gloves while handling)
4 teaspoons chopped garlic
$^1/_4$ cup chopped pearl onion
4 teaspoons chopped shallot
2 tablespoons each epazote and chives, chopped
4 banana leaves, approximately 12 inches square
oil in a spray bottle
4 chicken thighs or chicken breasts, skinless and boneless
salt and pepper

preparation

Mix the squash blossoms, chiles, garlic, onion, shallot, and herbs.

Spread out each banana leaf, and spray with oil. Arrange equal portions of the vegetables on each leaf, add a piece of chicken, and season with salt and pepper.

Seal up each package, and tie shut with a strip of banana leaf, if you have it.

Bake at 350 degrees F for 25 minutes, or steam for the same amount of time.

Serve on the banana leaf with all the cooking juices.

little secrets

You can successfully replace the banana leaves with 12 x 12-inch sheets of aluminum foil, the poblano chile with red bell pepper, and the epazote with parsley.

chicken with **mushrooms and spinach**

Serves 4

ingredients

8 sheets aluminum foil, 12 x 12 inches each
oil in a spray bottle
1 onion, diced
2 pounds fresh spinach, cut into strips
2 tablespoons each chopped basil, thyme,
oregano, and sage (preferably fresh), divided
4 boneless, skinless chicken breasts
1 pound mushrooms, thinly sliced
2 tablespoons white wine
salt and pepper

preparation

Arrange sheets of aluminum foil, two by two and crisscrossed, and spray them with oil.
Place on each set of foil: $1/4$ of the onion, $1/4$ of the spinach, $1/8$ of the herbs, one chicken breast, $1/4$ of the mushrooms, $1/4$ of the wine, and another $1/8$ of the herbs, seasoning with salt and pepper as you go.
Fold each piece of foil into a packet around the ingredients, and seal the ends well.
Steam or bake at 350 degrees F for 25 minutes.
Serve in the aluminum foil with all the cooking juices.

oriental chicken

Serves 6

ingredients

6 boneless, skinless chicken breasts
salt and pepper
1 onion, sliced
1 clove garlic, minced
flour
oil in a spray bottle
1 cup pineapple juice
$1/_4$ cup soy sauce
1 tablespoon white vinegar
3 tablespoons water
2 cups diced fresh or canned pineapple

preparation

Season the chicken breasts with salt and pepper, marinate for 20 minutes with the onion and garlic, and flour each one.
Spray a skillet with oil, and brown the chicken breasts.
Arrange the chicken in a baking dish with the pineapple juice, soy sauce, vinegar, water, and pineapple.
Bake at 350 degrees F just until the chicken is done, not letting it dry out.

little secrets

You can squeeze your own pineapple juice with a juicer, or you can purée the fruit in a blender and thin it with water.
Try this with mango instead of pineapple, and orange juice instead of pineapple juice.

veal with garden vegetables
. . . .

Serves 6

ingredients

oil in a spray bottle
6 veal cutlets
salt and pepper
2 large onions, diced
3 carrots, peeled and diced
3 ribs of celery, diced
12 cherry tomatoes, quartered
2 bay leaves
2 cups chicken broth
fresh thyme
grated zest of 1 lemon

preparation

Spray a skillet with oil, season the veal cutlets with salt and pepper, and brown them on both sides.

Add the onion, carrots, celery, tomatoes, and bay leaves, followed by the chicken broth, thyme, and lemon zest.

Cover and simmer over low heat, adding more broth if necessary to keep the veal moist.

braised veal

Serves 6

ingredients

2 pounds veal filet or other tender cut,
cubed
salt and pepper
flour
oil in a spray bottle
2 large onions, diced
2 green apples, diced
4 large, ripe tomatoes, peeled and diced
4 teaspoons curry powder
2 tablespoons paprika
2 cups chicken broth
4 potatoes, peeled and diced

preparation

Season the meat with salt and pepper and dredge with flour.

Spray a skillet with oil, and brown the meat.

Stir in the onion, apple, and tomatoes. Sauté for 5 minutes. Add the curry powder, paprika, and chicken broth.

Cover the pan and simmer over low heat until the veal starts to become tender. Uncover the pan, and add the potatoes. Continue to simmer until all ingredients are well cooked.

stuffed chiles with bean sauce

Serves 4

ingredients

4 poblano chiles, seeds and veins removed (wear gloves while handling)

stuffing

$1/2$ cup ricotta or cottage cheese
4 teaspoons Parmesan cheese
4 teaspoons peeled, chopped poblano chile
$1/4$ cup plain yogurt
salt and pepper

sauce

3 cups black beans, cooked with garlic, onion, and celery
3 tomatillos
1 serrano chile, roasted and peeled (wear gloves while handling)
epazote (a favorite Mexican herb for beans)
oil in a spray bottle
salt and pepper

preparation

Mix the cheeses, chopped poblano chile, and yogurt.
Season with salt and pepper.
Stuff the whole chiles with the cheese mixture.
Purée the beans, tomatillos, serrano chile, and epazote together.
Spray a skillet with oil, and in it lightly sauté the bean mixture for 15 minutes, adding water if necessary.
Add salt and pepper to taste.
Place the chiles in a baking dish, cover them with a bit of the bean sauce, and bake them at 325 degrees F for 15 minutes. Use the rest of the bean sauce to garnish each chile and its plate. Serve immediately.

little secret

Possible substitutions: bell pepper for poblano chile, parsley for epazote, and green tomatoes for tomatillos.

cheese **dumpling**

Serves 1

ingredients

1 cup cooked spaghetti, al dente
oil in a spray bottle

sauce

2 ripe tomatoes
1 clove garlic, peeled and slightly crushed
1 sprig each of fresh basil, thyme, and rosemary
salt and pepper

dumpling

$1/_2$ cup cottage cheese
1 tablespoon plain yogurt
2 sun-dried tomatoes, soaked for 8 hours in
$1/_4$ cup orange juice and 1 tablespoon olive oil
2 basil leaves, minced
salt and pepper
2 thin lengthwise slices of eggplant, with peel

preparation

To prepare the sauce, plunge the tomatoes in boiling water, peel and seed them, and dice the pulp. Spray a skillet with oil and add the garlic. Sauté the garlic and stir in the tomatoes, followed by the herbs. Season with salt and pepper, and add enough water to keep the sauce moist. Simmer for 15 minutes, then remove the garlic and herbs.

To make the dumpling, mix the cottage cheese, yogurt, drained and chopped sun-dried tomatoes, and basil. Season the mixture with salt and pepper, and set aside. Spray another skillet with oil, brown the eggplant slices, and arrange them in the shape of a cross in a small baking dish. Add the stuffing, enclosing it in the eggplant, and bake the dumpling at 350 degrees F for 15 minutes.

Arrange the hot spaghetti on a plate, add the tomato sauce, and serve with the dumpling on top.

little secret

For a garnish, try finely sliced eggplant skin, sautéed in a skillet sprayed with oil, and then arranged on top of the dumpling.

squash blossom and cheese crepes

Serves 2

ingredients

filling

oil in a spray bottle
$^{1}/_{2}$ cup minced onion
$^{1}/_{2}$ poblano chile, roasted, peeled, seeded,
deveined, and julienned (wear gloves to handle)
4 cups of squash blossoms, minced
salt and pepper
1 tablespoon minced cilantro
7 ounces Oaxaca cheese, grated (see "little
secrets" below)

sauce

10 ounces tomatillos
1 tablespoon chopped garlic
2 tablespoons chopped onion
1 tablespoon chopped chile (chilaca or poblano)
$1^{1}/_{2}$ cups water

crepes

oil in a spray bottle
4 egg whites
salt

preparation

Spray a skillet with oil, and sauté the onion and chile strips. Add the squash blossoms and sauté until they are cooked. Season with salt and pepper, and finally stir in the cilantro and grated cheese.

Purée together the tomatillos, garlic, onion, chopped chile, and a little salt for the sauce.

Spray another skillet with oil, and sauté the tomatillo purée for 5 minutes, then add the water and simmer until the sauce thickens.

Spray another skillet with oil. One by one, lightly beat each egg white with a little salt, and sauté, forming a crepe.

Fill the 2 crepes with the blossom mixture.

Pour half of the sauce into a baking dish, add the stuffed crepes, and pour the rest of the sauce on top.

Bake at 350 degrees F for 20 minutes.

little secrets

- In the crepe filling, use other vegetables such as eggplant, zucchini, spinach, or mushrooms.
- The tomatillo sauce may be replaced with tomato sauce or various chile sauces.
- Mozzarella, string, or other mild white cheese can stand in for the Oaxaca cheese.

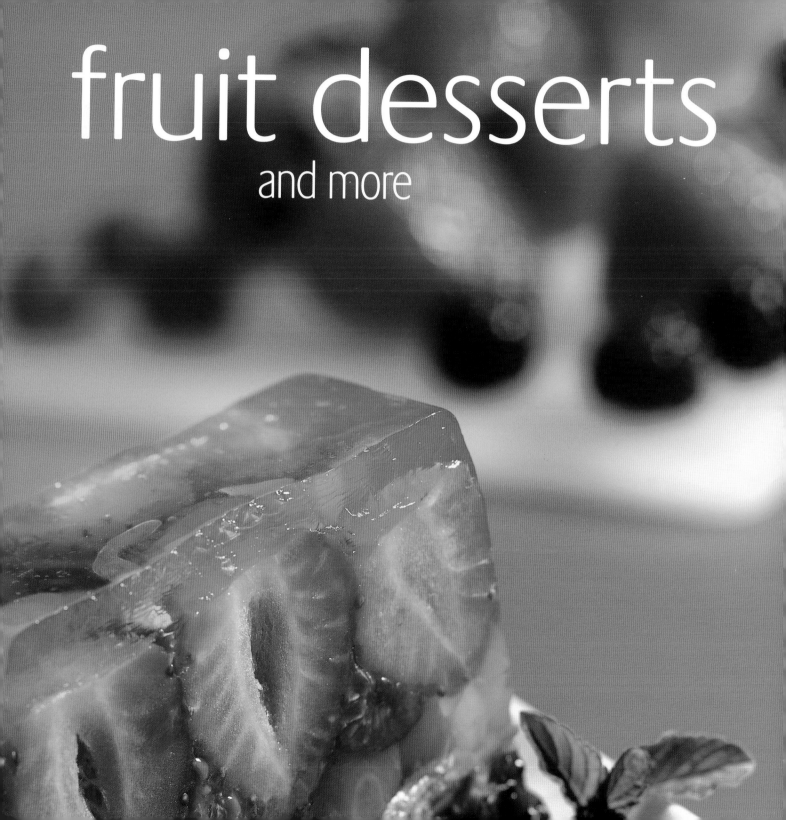

fruit desserts
and more

fruit desserts and more

little secrets

To achieve the finest texture in desserts made with unflavored gelatin, it is important to soak the gelatin first. This will moisten it and allow it to mix better with the other ingredients.

When you warm the gelatin (just before using it), never let it boil, because this will make it sticky. Powdered gelatin should soak for 10 minutes and then be gently warmed until the liquid is clear.
It's also a good idea to strain this reconstituted gelatin before cooking with it, to avoid any possible formation of lumps.

strawberry mousse

Serves 5

ingredients

2 envelopes ($^1/_2$ ounce total) unflavored gelatin
$^1/_2$ cup cold water
2 cups strawberry purée (from 10 ounces strawberries)
2 cups plain yogurt (not nonfat)
$^1/_3$ cup sugar, plus more to taste
oil in a spray bottle

preparation

Soak the gelatin in the cold water for 10 minutes. Then warm it slowly over low heat, and strain it.
Purée the strawberries, yogurt, sugar, and gelatin in a blender or food processor. Taste, and add more sugar if needed.
Pour the mixture into an oiled one-quart gelatin mold, and refrigerate until set.

little secrets

This is excellent served with fresh strawberries or strawberry sauce. (Simply purée more berries with sugar to taste.)
Mango makes a good substitute for strawberries.

sapodilla or plum gelatin with oranges

Serves 12

ingredients

3 envelopes ($^3/_4$ ounce total) unflavored gelatin, divided
2 cups cold water, divided
2 tablespoons sugar, or more to taste
1 teaspoon vanilla extract
oil in a spray bottle
2 oranges, peeled and sectioned
1$^1/_2$ cups orange juice
2 pounds sapodillas or plums, peeled and seeded
1 small package ($2^3/_4$–3 ounces) orange-flavored gelatin
1 cup boiling water
3 tablespoons orange marmalade

preparation

Soak 1 envelope of the unflavored gelatin in 1 cup of the cold water. After 10 minutes, gently warm and strain it, and add the sugar and the vanilla.

Pour half of this mixture into a large (3-quart) oiled gelatin mold. Wait until it begins to set, and then arrange the orange sections neatly around the mold. Add the rest of the gelatin mixture.

Refrigerate until set.

Dissolve the 2 remaining envelopes of unflavored gelatin in the orange juice, and let it rest for 10 minutes. Warm and strain.

Purée the sapodillas or plums.

Dissolve the orange-flavored gelatin in the boiling water, then add 1 cup of cold water, the puréed sapodillas or plums, and the marmalade. Stir in the gelatin-orange juice mixture.

Remove the mold from the refrigerator, add the second mixture, and refrigerate again until set.

sapodilla pears with orange sauce

Serves 4

ingredients

pears covered with sapodilla gelatin

2 cups peeled and seeded sapodillas or canned plums
4 cups water
$^1/_2$ cup sugar (or to taste)
2 envelopes ($^1/_2$ ounce total) unflavored gelatin, divided
4 whole peeled pears, with stems left on

sauce

1 pear, peeled, seeded, and diced
1 cup water
2 tablespoons orange marmalade
$^1/_2$ cup orange juice
1 tablespoon grated orange zest, rinsed in boiling water and drained
2 teaspoons minced candied ginger (optional)

preparation

Purée the sapodillas or plums with the water, then add sugar and bring to a boil. Lower the heat and simmer.
Sprinkle 1 envelope unflavored gelatin into this mixture, whisking vigorously, and then add the whole pears and poach them. When the pears are barely tender, remove them from the liquid.
Turn off the heat, and add the second envelope of gelatin as you did the first. Mix well.
Return the pears to the gelatin mixture and let them absorb it for 10 minutes, off heat. Then lift up each pear with a spoon, and use another spoon to coat it repeatedly with more of the gelatin mixture. Chill the pears. Refrigerate the remaining gelatin to eat or to use later.

sauce

Simmer the diced pear in the cup of water. When the pear is cooked, add the marmalade, orange juice, orange zest, and candied ginger. Simmer the sauce for a few minutes, then remove it from the heat, chill it, and purée it.
Serve the pears accompanied with the sauce.

fruit **crystal**

Serves 12

ingredients

2 cups strawberries
2 cups raspberries
2 cups blueberries
2 cups blackberries
2 cups seedless green grapes
zest of 4 oranges, cut into julienne matchsticks
4 envelopes (1 ounce total) unflavored gelatin
$1/_2$ cup water
4 cups orange juice
3 sprigs of fresh mint
$1/_4$ cup sugar, or to taste
4 slices candied ginger, minced (optional)
1 deep rectangular gelatin mold, 12-cup capacity,
or 2 large (9 x 5-inch) loaf pans, oiled

little
secrets
Accompany fruit crystal with a sauce made
of blackberries, kiwi fruit, or strawberries
simply puréed with a few drops of lemon
juice and powdered sugar to taste. You may
replace any of the fruits in the dessert with
melon, papaya, pear, mango, etc., shaped
with a melon baller.

preparation

Wash the fruit, and set aside some for decoration later. **Blanch** the orange zest in boiling water for 2 minutes, then drain it. **Soak** the gelatin in $1/_2$ cup water, and reserve. Bring the orange juice, mint, orange zest, and sugar to a boil and simmer for 1 minute. Strain this liquid, reserving the juice and the zest separately. **Heat** the soaked gelatin gently, strain it into the orange juice mixture, and stir to dissolve it well. Chill it until it begins to set. **Pour** a little of the gelatin into the oiled mold or molds. Make a layer of strawberries, then add the blueberries. Pour on a little more gelatin, and add the orange zest and the minced ginger. Repeat this procedure with the rest of the fruit, and finish with the remaining gelatin. **Cover** the mold or molds with aluminum foil, and weight the surface down with a board or something heavy to evenly compress the gelatin mixture. This will create a better cutting consistency later. **Refrigerate** the gelatin until it is firm. **Unmold** the dessert by dipping the pan in hot water and reversing it over a platter. **Cut** it into slices with a very sharp knife or an electric knife. Garnish with the reserved fruit and extra zest if desired.

apples with hibiscus flowers

Serves 2

ingredients

4 cups water
1 large box (6 ounces) strawberry gelatin
2 peeled apples, with stems still attached

sauce

2 cups water
$1/_2$ cup dried hibiscus flowers (see "little secrets" below)
$1/_4$ cup sugar, or to taste

preparation

Bring to a boil the 4 cups of water. Add the gelatin, whisking quickly. Then add the apples, and poach them at a simmer.
Once the apples are cooked, let them settle for 10 minutes, then remove them from the gelatin.
Refrigerate the remaining gelatin to eat or to use later.

sauce
Boil 2 cups of water with the hibiscus flowers and sugar for 20 minutes. Remove from heat, and chill. Serve the apples with the sauce.

little secrets

Flavorful hibiscus (called "jamaica" in Spanish) flowers are available in the tea section of many health-food stores, from Latin American food suppliers, or on the Internet.
If you prefer, you may substitute strawberry or raspberry sauce.

fruit baked in foil

Serves 2

ingredients

2 squares aluminum foil, 12 x 12 inches each
1 mango or large peach, peeled, pitted, and
cut into bite-sized cubes
1 green apple, peeled, cored, and cut into
bite-sized cubes
$1^{1}/_{2}$ cups halved strawberries or cherries
1 firm pear, peeled, cored, and cut into
medium cubes
2 tablespoons honey
2 tablespoons orange juice
$^{1}/_{4}$ teaspoon cinnamon
2 whole cloves

preparation

Distribute equal portions of the fruit between the two foil squares, and sprinkle with the honey, orange juice, and cinnamon. Add a clove to each portion.
Seal the foil tightly into packets. Place on a rimmed baking sheet.
Bake at 350 degrees F for 15 minutes.
Serve in the foil packets to retain all the cooking juices.

little secret

This is very good served slightly warm, accompanied with a scoop of ice cream.

orange **foam**

Serves 4

ingredients

1 envelope ($^1/_4$ ounce) unflavored gelatin
$^1/_2$ cup cold water
2 cups plain yogurt (not nonfat)
$^1/_4$ cup orange juice concentrate, thawed
$^1/_2$ teaspoon grated orange zest
1–2 tablespoons honey, or to taste

decoration

2 large navel oranges, cut in half and carefully hollowed out to make 4 "shells," reserving the fruit inside for decorative slices
$^1/_4$ cup honey

preparation

Soak the gelatin in the cold water for 10 minutes. Warm it gently, then strain it.

Purée together in the blender the yogurt, orange juice concentrate, orange zest, honey, and gelatin mixture.

Refrigerate in a bowl until the foam is set.

Fill the empty orange halves with the orange mixture.

Decorate with honey and reserved orange slices before serving.

hibiscus flower gelatin with mango sauce

Serves 4

ingredients

gelatin

3 cups water
$^3/_4$ cup dried hibiscus flowers (see "little secrets" on page 145)
$^1/_2$ cup sugar, or to taste
3 envelopes unflavored gelatin ($^3/_4$ ounce total)
$^1/_2$ cup cold water
1 mango, peeled, seeded, and cut into cubes
oil in a spray bottle

sauce

$^1/_2$ mango
1 tablespoon sugar, or to taste

preparation

Boil the water, hibiscus flowers, and sugar together. Strain and reserve the liquid.

Soak the gelatin in the cold water for 10 minutes. Later, gently heat until the gelatin dissolves, then strain it. Mix the gelatin with the hibiscus water and mango cubes.

Pour the mixture into an oiled one-quart mold, and refrigerate it.

To make the sauce, purée the mango with the sugar.

pear and sweet potato tart

Serves 3

ingredients

8 ounces sweet potatoes
1 pear, peeled, cored, and cut into large dice
1 tablespoon honey, or to taste
$1/_2$ cup water
$1/_2$ cup plain yogurt
2 egg whites, divided
1 tablespoon sugar, or to taste

preparation

Boil the sweet potatoes, then purée them in a blender with a little of the cooking water.

Cook the pear in a small pan with honey and water, until juice has completely reduced and pear has caramelized.

Mix the sweet potato purée with the yogurt and one of the egg whites.

Fill 3 individual ramekins with this mixture, and add pears.

Bake at 350 degrees F for 20 minutes. Whip remaining egg white until soft peaks form, and gradually add the sugar. Taste and add more if necessary. Beat until stiff peaks form.

Remove the ramekins from the oven, add the meringue, and bake again until they are golden brown. Serve cold.

apple and ricotta **delight**

Serves 6

ingredients

3 apples, peeled, cored, and diced
3 tablespoons honey, or to taste
2 cups water
oil in a spray bottle
3 tablespoons brown sugar, or to taste
3 cups ricotta cheese
3 eggs
1 tablespoon vanilla extract

preparation

Cook the apples in a small saucepan with the honey and the water, until the apples are tender, the water is completely reduced, and the apples have caramelized. More water may be necessary.

Spray a 10-inch baking dish or pan with oil, and sprinkle it with brown sugar.

Mix the ricotta cheese until it is completely smooth, and mix in the eggs and the vanilla.

Arrange the apples in the baking dish, topping them with the cheese mixture.

Bake at 350 degrees F for 20 minutes.

Unmold while warm. Serve cold.

mango smoothie

Serves 2

ingredients

1 large plump mango, peeled and diced
1 cup plain yogurt
sugar or honey to taste (optional)

preparation

Put 2 goblets into the freezer.
Blend the mango and the yogurt together in the blender.
Sweeten to taste.
Pour the mixture into the goblets, and chill before serving.

meringue nests with fruit and cream

Serves 4

ingredients

for the meringue

1 egg white
1 pinch cream of tartar
$^1/_4$ cup sugar

for the home-style cream

$^1/_4$ cup low-fat milk
$^1/_4$ teaspoon unflavored gelatin
1 tablespoon cold water
$^1/_2$ cup plain yogurt
1 tablespoon sugar

your choice of fruit to fill the nests

preparation

Whip the egg white at low speed for several minutes until it is foamy. Add the cream of tartar and sprinkle in the sugar, beating at high speed for 10 minutes more.

Form 4 meringue nests (see photograph) on a baking sheet lined with parchment paper, and bake at 250 degrees F for 40 minutes or until they are very dry and crisp.

For the home-style cream, pour the milk into a glass container, and freeze until ice crystals begin to form (approximately 40 minutes).

Soak the gelatin in the tablespoon of cold water for 10 minutes.

Remove the milk from the freezer.

Warm the gelatin gently, then strain it into the milk, stirring.

Add the yogurt and sugar.

Beat the cream until it forms stiff peaks.

Chill it for 15 minutes in the refrigerator.

Fill the meringue nests with the cream and your choice of fruit.

coffee **flan**

Serves 6

ingredients

2 cups low-fat milk
1 tablespoon instant espresso coffee, or to taste
2 tablespoons sugar, or to taste
1 envelope ($^1/_4$ ounce) unflavored gelatin
$^1/_2$ cup cold water
1 cup plain yogurt (or 1 cup coffee-flavored yogurt)
oil in a spray bottle

preparation

Warm the milk, then add the coffee and sugar. Taste, and add more of each if you like.

Soak the gelatin in the cold water for 10 minutes, then gently warm it.

Strain the gelatin into the milk and coffee mixture, and stir in the yogurt.

Spray 6 ramekins or a one-quart mold with oil, and fill them with the flan mixture.

Refrigerate until it sets.

Unmold after first dipping each mold into hot water, and serve.

little secret

You may like to accompany this flan with the home-style cream from page 158.

apricot dessert

· · · · · · · · · · · ·

Serves 6

ingredients

7 ounces dried apricots
6 cups cold water, divided
1 large box (6 ounces) peach gelatin (or orange or lemon)

preparation

Simmer the apricots in 4 cups of water until they are tender.
Reserve 2 cups of the cooking water.
Prepare the peach gelatin with the hot reserved cooking water, plus 2 cups cold water, and refrigerate until the gelatin begins to set.
Remove the half-congealed gelatin from the refrigerator.
Purée the apricots, add the gelatin, and return the mixture to the refrigerator until completely set.

did you **know?**

al dente
Refers to the degree of cooking that a food should have to be soft on the outside and firm on the inside.

ancho chile
This wide (about 3 by 5 inches), dry, reddish-brown pepper is very common in Mexico. It ranges from mild to quite hot, and its flavor is deep and rich.

basil
An herb often used in Mediterranean and Thai cuisine; it's the herb par excellence for seasoning tomatoes and pasta.

bay leaf
The dried leaves of the laurel tree, used in moderation, add a subtle aroma to dishes cooked long and slowly, to stuffings, and to marinades.

banana leaves
Large, flavorful wrappers for many steamed or baked Latin American dishes. Remove the stems and center veins (save these for tying) and heat the leaves to make them more flexible.

chilaca chile
Chilacas are long, thin, hot peppers, blackish-green in color, which are often served peeled and seeded.

chive
Seasoning for various dishes, hot as well as cold. Chives are best raw, so add them at the last moment.

cilantro (coriander)
Used in Mexican cooking to enrich the flavor of soups, salsas, sauces, salads, and stews.

cinnamon
Mexican cinnamon, called canela, is much milder than the cinnamon widely available in the U.S. The recipes in this book have been adjusted accordingly.

clove
It tastes spicy and "hot" and resembles a tiny metal nail; it enhances marinades and desserts.

curry
The name for a mixture of spices. Basic to Indian cuisine, it tastes "hot" and appears in meat and vegetable dishes as well as soups and sauces.

epazote
This pungent leafy herb is common in southern Mexican cooking, especially to flavor black beans.

fennel
Used in Italian cooking as both a vegetable and a flavoring, the taste of fennel is slightly sweet and reminiscent of anise.

guajillo chile
Also called chiles traviesos, or "mischievous chiles," because of their bite, guajillos are almost as versatile and popular as anchos, but guajillos taste fruitier and more dynamic.

ginger
The pulp of this root is very aromatic and spicy. It is a basic ingredient in many Asian cuisines, enhancing sauces, meats, fish, soups, and marinades.

julienne
This is a way of cutting food into matchstick-thin strips. Vegetables cook evenly and rapidly when julienned.

lemongrass
Actually a member of the grass family, this herb is cultivated in warm, moist climates for its aromatic lemon-like oil, used in cooking as well as in cosmetics and insect repellents.

maguey leaves
Magueys are edible succulents most famous for being distilled into tequila. The inner transparent lining, or "veil," can be stripped from the leaf and used as a wrapper for steamed foods. Banana leaves or foil make acceptable substitutes.

marjoram
The scent and flavor of this herb are reminiscent of mint and basil. Marjoram enhances vinegars, fish dishes, and meats.

mint
This herb adds flavor to vegetables, meats, and desserts.

nutmeg
Combining well with dairy products, nutmeg also flavors potatoes, eggs, cheese, sauces, and desserts.

oregano
Indispensable herb in Mediterranean cuisine, particularly in recipes containing tomatoes.

paprika
Red bell pepper, dried and ground. It is used with eggs, poultry, shellfish, and fresh cheese.

parsley
This herb is ideal for enriching the flavor of soups and stews, and to use as a garnish.

poblano chile
Large, triangular fresh green chiles, very popular peeled and stuffed, poblanos have a wide range of piquancy. When ripened and dried, they become anchos.

prickly pear pads (nopales)
The young, tender, paddle-shaped stems of the prickly pear cactus. After their spines are removed, they may be diced and cooked in many ways and taste a bit like green beans.

purslane (verdolagas)

Flourishes in the wild and is even considered a weed in American gardens. Its unique taste and texture add much to salads. Substitute other tangy greens such as escarole, chicory, or watercress.

rosemary

This herb has a strong perfume that enriches stuffings, soups, sauces, and marinades.

saffron

Buy saffron in the form of threads, not powder, and let it soak in a hot liquid before adding it to food. (Saffron is the most expensive of all spices.)

sage

Its flavor is sharp; it is used with white meats, soups, and sauces.

sapodilla (zapote)

A tropical fruit also called Mexican custard apple, marmalade plum, and chocolate pudding fruit, names that hint at the many different varieties. Possible substitutes: plum, prune, persimmon, peach, or mango.

serrano chile

These crisp inch-long green peppers are eaten either fresh, cooked, or pickled. Their seeds and veins are very hot, and their flesh has a strong, snappy flavor.

tarragon

Aromatic plant with the flavor of anise, slightly bitter and piquant.

thyme

An aromatic, twiggy plant, thyme is a favorite ingredient in stews, soups, and tomato sauces.

tomatillos

Not an unripe tomato, but a different plant altogether, the tart apple-green tomatillo grows beneath a papery husk, which must be removed before cooking. Tomatillos are prized for making sauces.

to blend

To mix carefully without beating.

to fillet

To cut meat in thin slices.

to marinate

To set a food to soak in wine, spices, or oil to flavor, preserve, or soften it.

to reduce

To boil down a sauce or stock, concentrating its flavor and texture by means of evaporation.

Also available from Rio Nuevo Publishers:

Clouds for Dessert: Sweet Treats from the Wild West

by Susan Lowell

The Prickly Pear Cookbook

by Carolyn Niethammer

Flora's Kitchen: Recipes from a New Mexico Family

by Regina Romero

Southwest Kitchen Garden

by Kim Nelson

www.rionuevo.com